Yes, I Must Admit We Are Neighbors

By Duane Anderson

For my sophomore English teacher,
Bruce Bothwell, who got me interested in writing poetry.

Acknowledgements

Carcinogenic Poetry   Where's the Pooch?

Cholla Needles   Autumn: One Against One; Sharing
          Neighbors; Too Perfect

Dual Coast   Most People Mow Their Weeds;
          Dueling Lawn Mowers

Fine Lines   Second Chance; Listening to the
          Squirrel; Late Night Visitor; Unofficial
          Newspaper Carrier

Indiana Voice Journal Revenge of the Red Sunset Maple

October Hill Magazine Lost and Found

Poesis Literary Journal Final Resting Spot; The Life of a
          Dandelion; Model Neighbor

Scarlet Leaf Review   The Adventures of the Crooked
          Walker

Sincerely Magazine   Beginning of Autumn

Tipton Poetry Journal My Name is Neighbor

Contents

Model Neighbor

I wasn't being very neighborly today,
I stayed indoors, but I blamed it on the hot humid
weather as being the culprit for me staying inside.

I preferred the cool circulation of an air conditioned
house to the steamy and muggy outdoors,
and I didn't feel like using the free sauna

that was available from nature today.
I guess I can be very picky sometimes,
then again, maybe I was being neighborly,

for I wasn't bothering anyone today, not
that anyone has ever told me in person that
I was a pest and had caused them trouble before.

As far as I was concerned, I was the model
neighbor, just ask me, and I will tell you so.
I still even have the good neighbor seal

of approval that I gave to myself,
all framed and proudly displayed on
my living room wall.

Mr. Poop

Every once in awhile
I walk my dog
past Mr. Poop's yard for a change of pace.
He has a sign in his front yard that states:
"I don't poop in your yard,
so don't poop in mine!!!"

How do I know that he
doesn't poop in my yard?
Every once in awhile
poop mysteriously shows up
in my front yard
and I know it isn't from my dog.
How do I know that Mr. Poop
didn't do this.
Should I believe him
just because I didn't see
him do it
or should I take him at his word
that he didn't do it?

Maybe I should set up a security camera
to see who is doing it
or I could put up a sign like his.
Then I would be called Mr. Poop II,
and I don't need that added to my resume.
I have had a few nicknames over the years,
some that I liked
and some I didn't care for,
but I will let him continue to hold
the title of Mr. Poop.

The Adventures of the Crooked Walker

Each morning I see her as I walk my dog.
I call her the crooked walker.
She, in her purple top and black shorts,
never altering her outfit from day to day.
She walks forward
going from one side of the sidewalk
to the other side
as she does her daily walk.

I vary the route I take
when I am walking my dog.
She walks the same route
the same six blocks
back and forth multiple times
though I am never around long enough
to tally the count.

My mind wanders
as I walk,
wondering if she ever had gotten
pulled over by the police while driving her car,
and if the officer asked her
to walk a straight line,
could she do it?

Where's the Pooch?

Today I was asked twice,
where's the pooch,
where's your dog,
as I took a walk alone.
People were used to seeing me
with my dog
since I usually took her on
two to three walks a day
depending on the weather.
We were a well known
neighborhood staple.
One wasn't seen without the other.

Now I can only tell them as they ask
that she is no longer alive
having lost the use of both hind legs
due to a disc disease.
I continue my walks.
Maybe not as many
though the pace is much faster now
since I have no need or desire
to sniff at every little thing crossing my path.
We were a twosome,
one of the threads of the neighborhood.
As life moves on,
the memories remain.

My Name Is Neighbor

From time to time,
Which I didn't see very often,
one neighbor in particular,
this wasn't often,
would just say 'Hi Neighbor'
like it was my name.
He never called me by my first name
though I was pretty sure I had one.
Maybe he just didn't care to know it
or maybe he couldn't remember my name,
and I never bothered to ask.

To him I had a name,
it was Neighbor,
though at least he remembered
I was one of his neighbors,
but still, it made me wonder if he called all
his neighbors by the same name.
It sure would simplify his life.

Assisted Suicide

I didn't know, nor did I ask
but for whatever reason our new neighbors
did not care about the health
of the grass in their yard.
The sun punished the grass each day
as temperatures reached the high nineties
and even triple digit heat,
but our neighbors provided the grass
with no refreshing beverage.

Their sprinkler system was working
earlier in the year before
the prior neighbors sold the house and
moved away elsewhere to parts unknown.
So now the yard is completely brown
and they can claim that they along with the sun
assisted in the suicide of their grass.
No longer do they have to mow it,
and the grass lies in its final resting spot
where there will be no funeral service or proper burial.

Beginning of Autumn

Now that there is no longer
a tree in our backyard,
this fall I only have
our neighbor's tree to contend with,
and the winds are doing a great job
of blowing its leaves into our yard.

I wish the winds would blow
in a different direction,
but I know that isn't going to happen,
at least for today.
In the meantime,
the leaves pile up

and some time in the near future
I will have to deal with them,
and when I rake the leaves up,
I will think of the good times
when our tree too cooperated with the wind
and sent little packages of its own

into our neighbor's yard.
Though I am glad I no longer
have to rake the thousands of leaves
that our old tree once produced,
I only miss the beauty of the tree,
which now only exists in my memories.

Revenge of the Red Sunset Maple

For reasons unknown, our Red Sunset Maple
didn't seem to like the pruning
done to it last fall,
and when spring rolled around,
it got its revenge
by scattering thousands of seeds
all over our backyard.
Years ago, the man at the nursery
where we purchased this tree
said that it was a seedless maple.
This was pretty much true
for the first ten years,
but this year the tree had its revenge.

So as of late, I have become a lumberjack
dressed in my plaid flannel shirt, blue jeans with suspenders
singing lumberjack songs
as I pull up thousands of these little trees
developed from these seeds.
Maybe my neighbors think I am a strange one,
but it doesn't matter because I am.
As I pull up the little trees scattered over the yard,
I contemplate about how I can become
friends again with the tree,
after all,
I do enjoy the shade it provides.

Most People Mow Their Weeds

In some neighborhoods, the home owners cut their grass,
but in our neighborhood, most people mow their weeds.
Some might call them invasive weeds,
but to a few too many neighbors,
they seem to be welcomed,
the crab grasses, the water grasses, the foxtail grasses.
All of them have the names of various grasses,
so welcome, welcome, welcome they say.
Yes, the other yards are mostly green,
except for maybe the yellow dandelions
popping up all over the yard,
or a field of clover with their white flowers,
or the bull thistle, or yellow wood sorrel.
The list of weeds goes on and on.

Their whole yard is part of a flower garden,
and these, the flowers in their flowerbed,
requiring very little attention,
and to tell the truth, none at all.
You won't see any of the neighbors picking any
of the flowers to place on their dinner table.
No, there is no time for that.
Instead, they leave them alone
for everyone else in the neighborhood to enjoy.
In the meantime, while they mow their weeds,
maybe weekly, maybe every once in awhile,
I will continue to cut my grass.
I guess I'm old fashioned that way.

Dueling Lawn Mowers

They had matching lawn mowers.
She mowed the front yard,
and he mowed the back.
It reminded me of the movie *Deliverance*
where I first heard the song *Dueling Banjos*
at the beginning of the movie
where a young boy playing a banjo
dueling an older man playing a guitar.
Why they called it *Dueling Banjos*
I never quite understood since one of the instruments
definitely wasn't any banjo I was use to seeing.

We have also seen dueling pianos,
where two pianists trying to outdo each other,
and dueling pistols where
one of both didn't survive the outcome,
but dueling lawn mowers,
that is definitely a new one on me.

Yes, I'm sure it gets the lawn mowed faster,
so now I am waiting for them to
finish with their lawn mower routine
to see if they break out
dueling weed whackers to trim
the grasses along the foundation of the house
and along the fence.

And then I wonder
if they also have dueling vacuums
for cleaning the carpets inside their house.
Dueling,
the options are unlimited it seems.

Car Lot People

Somehow these neighbors liked their vehicles
with two cars in the garage,
three others in the driveway,
and two along the side of their house.
No matter how many times I walked by
it always looked like they were having a party
or maybe had a large family
with several children old enough to drive,
except I had only ever seen the two of them,
a husband and wife living in the house.

Another observation about the vehicles,
as strange as it may be,
was that they only seemed to use three of them.
The other four vehicles didn't ever seem to get moved,
so why did they have them, maybe for show,
but still the reason remains unknown.
So I assigned them a name of my own making.
I call them the Car Lot people
since I do not know their names,
and they live several blocks from me.

They could be storing some of the cars
for some friends and relatives I guess,
but if they do, I can only hope
they charge enough for their troubles,
especially in winter when they scrape
the frost off the windows, or brush the snow off
and get into a cold car.

Whatever the reason for having all the vehicles,
it is a part of their life and choosing.
As for me, I choose to keep the car I drive
safely in our garage each night.
I too have my own priorities.

The Neighborhood Pilot

He wasn't your usual airplane pilot
as his plane flew high over my head.
There were no passengers or a flight crew
taking care of things on board,
and I wasn't so sure of his pilot skills
after I had last seen him trying to get
his plane out of the tree branches
where he had crashed it into.

His plane was only eight to twelve inches long,
so that is probably why no one was on board.
I noticed him several times before
when taking my walk through the neighborhood,
him sitting on his lawn chair
in his front yard with a controller in his hands
flying his aircraft.

After that last crash, I never saw
our pilot fly his plane again.
It could have been he was not able
to make the necessary repairs to
rebuild or purchase a replacement.
Then again, it could have been that I didn't
time my walks just right
to catch him in the act again.

Maybe he got a drone for Christmas
and is waiting for warmer weather
before he attempts another flight.
This is the control tower, over and out.

Clearing the Snow with Warm Weather

Each time it snows
I am outside wearing my winter coat, gloves,
and hat along with my shovel clearing the snow
away from the sidewalk and driveway,
and when nature coats the walks with ice
from a freezing rain,
once again I am outside,
not with a shovel but with my ice melt

spreading it around like I am
sowing seeds of grass on a naked lawn,
not wanting anyone
to slip, slide, or fall down
on the slick surface
as neighbors go out to walk their dogs
or kids walking to school.
Other neighbors tend to disagree with me

in the use of these tools, instead using
a different means of clearing their walks,
waiting on the warm weather
to melt away the snow and ice
no matter how long it may take.
They seem to have little concern for those
who wish for a safe walk, and I too am not one
who favors slipping or sliding on slick

sidewalks having had my share of falls.
I choose the safest path,

whether it is walking on cleared sidewalks
or walking on the snow covered grass
instead of using the intended sidewalk.
With age and experience,
sometimes comes common sense,
now just tell that to my other neighbors.

Neighborhood Feeder

Our neighbors set out several bird feeders
in their front and back yard.
Sure, the birds were getting their share of the bird seed,

but there weren't any signs in place
stating that squirrels were banned, and even if
there were one in place, I doubt any of them

could have read the sign, other than maybe
Rocket J. Squirrel, after all it wasn't like they had any
schools where the squirrels learned the English language.

The squirrel was just tending to one of its
basic needs of a little food for an empty stomach.
After it finishes dining, maybe it will

jump over to the bird bath
to wash down the meal with a little water.
As the squirrel continues with its snack,

several birds wait on the fence nearby
waiting for their turn with the bird seed,
but decide against waiting very long

and fly away, maybe to a different feeder.
A short time later, a rabbit likewise stops on by,
munching on some of the seed dropped by the squirrel.

It, not having the climbing abilities of the squirrel,
seemed quite content with the scraps left below.
This seemed to be the new neighborhood gathering spot.

I too might have gone over to it,
but I am not very fond of sunflower seeds, and besides,
the smaller seeds tend to stick between my teeth.

Autumn: One Against One

He started counting the leaves
falling from the tree
but stopped at one,
not that he couldn't count any higher
or became bored by his counting,
but it was one enormous pile,
spread all over the yard
and he knew that if he cleaned up this pile
there would be another to take its place
until finally the tree ran out of leaves.

Yes, one,
that is the final count.
One tree,
and right now it is winning
as he raked the leaves
in days past
trying to keep up with it.

He knows he will win in the end.
It is just a matter of time
before the tree runs out of ammunition,
but for now,
it is having a good time
watching him with his rake
and trash containers.
He is winning the war.
It's just that he had lost a few battles
and had to clean up after the skirmishes.

Meal Time

The squirrel hopped into the yard,
climbed the chain link fence,
and then performed a tight rope act

as it walked on top of the fence railing.
Nearing its intended destination,
it jumped off and continued

its journey to the bird feeder where
some bird seed had fallen to the ground.
The seed was just one of today's meals since

the acorns buried from last autumn could
have been all gone by now, or at least
forgotten where they all had been buried

having hidden so many last fall.
The meal was abruptly interrupted
when the neighbor closest to

where the bird feeders stood began
trimming the grass along the fence,
scaring the squirrel to the nearest tree.

I'm sure it will be back as soon as
things calm down again, knowing the
hunger won't go away on its own.

Watering the Neighbors' Yards

I am watering the yard today.
I had planned on putting down a grub
control application on the lawn instead, but
the instructions said to apply it on a dry lawn,

and the grass sure wasn't dry now.
The rain was coming down very hard along
with the roaring thunder doing its own thing.
Like I said, I'm watering the lawn and

I am very generous in sharing all this rain water
with everyone else in the neighborhood,
just to let you know that I wasn't
trying to be a tight wad or stingy

and was only doing it to my own yard,
though the best thing yet was knowing that
the water company wouldn't be billing me
for even a drop of this water.

I guess I will have to wait until tomorrow
to start the task I had intended doing today
after the grass has had a chance to dry out
from all my watering.

Yes, I am taking credit for the rain
coming down today and also all of the
blame from others who wished the rain
hadn't fallen and ended up spoiling their day.

Naming Rights

Some neighbors seem to give their dogs strange
names, and if the name wasn't already strange
enough, I may give them another name of my
own choosing. One in particular named their

two dogs Biscuit and Simba, but instead of
calling one of them by its given name of Simba
which sounded more like a cat's name
than a dog's name. I called her Gravy.

Biscuit and Gravy sounded better together,
like part of a tasty morning breakfast.
Another neighbor called their four dogs by the
seasons, Autumn, Winter, Spring and Summer,

but since they were new to the neighborhood, I
was still unable to keep all the seasons straight.
Even in our own family, our daughter named
three of her pets all starting with the letter 'C'.

I guess each of us has our own method of
naming things. If I were going to name a dog
I would probably call it Trouble, for I seemed
to be always getting into trouble.

After all, it was my middle name,
given to me by my loving parents
who knew years in advance on
how I would turn out to be in life.

Son of Elmer Fudd

He told me that he had shot four
rabbits in his yard so far this spring
with a pellet rifle because he was tired
of them destroying some of his flowers,

chewing the stems in half,
but not eating what they cut off.
He wasn't hunting them for their meat
for his next dinner meal of Hasenpfeffer.

They were just pests, like a rat or mouse
were to others. I imagined him wearing a
hunting hat like Elmer Fudd wore in the Bugs
Bunny cartoons as he continued his rambling,

even though Elmer was never successful at
catching a rabbit. He also said he had permission
from several of the neighbors to shoot them,
but I was not one of those neighbors he asked.

I always liked watching the rabbits from
our deck, though now that I think about it,
I hadn't seen any one in our yard for some time,
now knowing the reason why.

Elmer Fudd's son seemed to be very
successful in his hunting based on his own
boasting to me. I guess he didn't have to deal
with that rascally wabbit like his father did.

Late Night Visitor

The morning after the rain storm
I found half of a black walnut shell
on the deck in the back of the house.

I imagined some hungry squirrel wanted
a late night snack last evening choosing
one small section of our deck where

a two-foot overhang stuck out from the
roof providing it some protection from
the rain. I guessed that its home of

small branches and leaves was sopping
wet after several days of heavy rains. It
looked like the squirrel was successful with

its meal since I didn't see any meat left
in the shell that was left behind on the deck.
Even though it didn't have an invitation

from me to come into my house where it
was nice and dry and where I lived in
comfort, I had no problem with the squirrel

using the deck when I was inside the house,
though I wish it would at least clean up
after itself when it was through eating.

Second Chance

Off in the distance, a short
distance from where I sat,
only two houses away,
the neighbor's tree
stands naked of any leaves,
but not because it is autumn

and all the leaves had left its
branches for winter.
No, the branches are bare
because the tree's life had ended,
part of nature where nothing lives
forever, not man, not tree.

It was not coming back to life,
so I said a prayer as they,
cut it down, then chopped it up
to be used as firewood,
something not all get a chance at
doing, given a second purpose in life.

Abandoned Bird Feeder

The bird feeder in the neighbor's back
yard sits empty, hanging from the tree.
It has been abandoned

with no one to keep it filled with seed.
No birds land on the perch of the feeder
in order to fill its beak with a few seeds,

nor do squirrels drop down from
the branch from which it dangles.
It just hangs from the tree,

swinging back and forth with the wind,
no longer serving its intended
purpose as it once performed.

Its owners who placed it from the tree
years ago are no longer taking care of it.
It hangs from the empty branch,

now just a distant memory
of what once was alive and
bristling with activity.

Listening to the Squirrel

The squirrel is talking,
but I do not know who it is talking to
or what it is saying since I am
not familiar with its language

and I am not sure how I could learn it
if it truly is a language
and not just the sounds it makes
letting everyone know where it is.

I guess I am content that I am
knowledgeable in one language,
knowing that I could never learn
all the languages spoken on earth,

let alone all in the animal world.
Was it telling everyone with ear
shout that it was in the tree
and wanted no other visitors or

just liked to hear it chatter?
Now the squirrel has stopped making its
sounds, and I still have no clue
why it made the sounds it did.

Though I could not see the squirrel
with all the leaves covering its
place in the tree, and I knew
my place was not in the tree with it

due to a lack of climbing skills like the
squirrel and my fear of heights. I will let the
squirrel rule the tree world and continue
my listening as it makes the sounds it does.

Dog Pasture

Being in the city,
we didn't have any cow pastures nearby,
but we did live next to a dog pasture.
The neighbor next door had a herd of

dogs that was part of his family and were
not being raised to be sold for their meat.
Though the dogs didn't eat the grass
like cows tended to do, they did do

their own number with the grass,
wearing it so thin that only dirt appeared
in several spots within the yard,
and then there were the dog piles,

the many mounds that they left behind
on their adventures outside each day.
Today I was acting like a weatherman
as I sat on the deck reading my book.

It was hot and humid with a slight breeze,
blowing from a southerly direction,
definitely the wrong direction from where
I was sitting. It was then I knew it was time

for me to go inside, the outdoor scents were no
longer pleasing to the nose. There was no way the
flowers on the deck could compete with the smell
coming from next door, no matter hard they tried.

Uninvited Guest

The fly entered the house like it
was a member of the household,
bursting in when I opened the door

to go into the house, not knowing that
it had snuck in behind me before the door
closed shut. It was much later when I first

saw our uninvited guest as it circled around
the room checking the layout of the house,
or maybe just searching for a way to get

back out. As it came closer to the storm
door, I opened it up and out it flew which
was a much better option for it than

the alternative of me using the fly swatter
when it became tired and rested on a
wall or some flat area within the house

allowing me to give it a swat.
The fly won this time, unknowingly
making a very wise decision.

The Lonely Deck

I am not sure if they were thinking that
if they built a deck, then they will come,
hoping that friends and relatives would
come in flocks to be entertained on their deck,

but that might mean that they first had to
be invited. Maybe they were thinking it
would add to the value of their home if
they ever decided on selling the house,

or they just had some extra cash sitting around
and it sounded like a good idea at the time,
or maybe it was built so there would be
less lawn to mow in the backyard.

The deck stretched over half the length of the
house, built with two benches, two sets of steps,
but left undecorated with the usual deck furniture
like it was never intended on getting used.

Many years have now gone by since first constructed,
still standing next to the house going unused
like the patio before it, covered with cobwebs,
growing older along with the house, in boredom.

The Right Height

After reaching the height of five feet,
our neighbor finally cut down some weeds
in her back yard. Maybe it wasn't worth the effort
to her unless they reached a certain height.

Maybe she could no longer see over them,
so it was finally time to say goodbye to the weeds,
or it could have been she finally noticed
them growing in front of the tomato plants

after all this time when checking to see if
there were any ripe tomatoes ready for picking.
There are still a few weeds remaining,
but I take it they haven't reached

the mandatory height requirement yet.
Then right in the corner of their yard,
next to where two fences intersect,
stands a maple tree as it continues its growth.

It too is now taller than the fence having
grown from a seed from the tree next door.
Maybe one day she will also become a lumberjack after
discovering its existence too behind the tomato plants.

Night World

Sit down on the front steps
and look out to what lies out there.
Another house,
with neighbors on the front steps
looking across the street,
cars on the freeway
with passengers waving
not to say goodbye
or hello,
but see you later maybe.

Maybe the world will be seen
if a look is taken.
Outside, more is going on.
Get out of the house and
sit on the front steps for awhile.
Maybe a man will be sitting on top
of a flagpole wearing nothing but
his existence of knowledge knowing
that he is alive.
See a sunset.
See the moon come out of nowhere.
See the world come out of a faucet.
Take a drink.

The Gathering Place Goes Quiet

One can tell when the bird feeders haven't
been replenished with seed for awhile.
Birds make no attempt at landing on

the rungs of the feeders, nor go anywhere
near, knowing that there was nothing there
for them to feed on, and even the

neighborhood squirrels no longer come for
a visit. I missed all the activity from the next
door neighbor's yard when I went outside

to sit on the deck, knowing they had probably
already found another source for their seed,
so maybe I will have to go out and purchase

a couple feeders for our yard, along with
a good supply of seed to see if any will
return to the area again for me to watch.

Weed Freak 101

During the summer, I walk along the perimeter
of the fence in our back yard, looking for
any weeds that had crossed over from the
neighbors' yards into ours, trying to keep
our yard weed free, an action considered

necessary by me to keep it remaining that way,
for I had no intention of invading their yards in order
to clean up all of the weeds in their lawns,
especially one yard in particular, which would
definitely be a full-time job for several days.

Patrolling the perimeter was like being a prison guard,
though they were looking to keep the prisoners in,
while I was looking to keep unwanted things out.
In addition to this weekly routine, when mowing my
own lawn, I looked for other uninvited guests that

took hold in the yard, pulling them out as I
went along, and also monitored the tall weeds
and tomato plants growing through the fence,
sometimes pulling them back through to the side
where they belonged in their respective yards,

the birth where their roots originally took hold,
while other times, just whacking them off with the weed
whacker as I trimmed the grass growing along the fence.
Yes, I'm one of those neighbors who cares about his lawn,
I am one of those weed freaks, that's who I am.

Lost and Found

I am surprised what I sometimes find
on my walks through the neighborhood,
miniature drones, shopping carts,
discarded shoes, forgotten coats,

pennies, dimes, quarters, dollar bills, and yes,
even counterfeit one hundred-dollar bills.
Today, it was an arrow laying on the sidewalk.
I looked around and didn't see any

other arrows or a bow nearby, and William Tell,
Robin Hood, or Green Arrow were not in sight,
so those were good signs that I may be safe because
in some neighborhoods one hears of gun shots

being fired, and here, silent arrows fly through
the air. I only hope that their only destination
is the bullseye on a target, and not in a heart,
unless that arrow is shot by Cupid?

Johnny Oakseed

The squirrels were out in full force,
four of them under two pin oak trees.
It was harvest time, and they were busy
picking up the fallen acorns with their teeth,
going yard to yard burying them beneath
the ground to store their abundant
harvest for the upcoming winter season.

They were the Johnny Appleseeds of the
oak trees, but instead of carrying bags of
apple seeds, they carried acorns in
their mouths, planting them at multiple
locations throughout the neighborhood,
where oak trees sprouted up every spring from
those acorns long left forgotten from winter.

Attack of the Pirate Bugs

Even though it was a beautiful day,
the pirate bugs convinced me that
I really didn't want to be outside

sitting on the deck reading my book.
I couldn't determine if they wore eyepatches
and carried swords because of their tiny size,

and I, without my magnifying glass or microscope
to check those things out. They flew over to
meet me, not all at once, but several at a time,

though they had the strangest way of greeting me,
by biting me anywhere my skin was exposed,
and the bite for their size was definitely annoying.

After several dozen had landed on me, having only been
outside for just a few minutes, and they taking on a few
casualties of their own from me swatting them as they landed,

I had had enough, and called it quits, going back
inside to a place where I hoped I was free from them.
They had been very persuasive, and had won this round.

In another day, I may try it again,
hoping to find a day of peace where
they are raiding some other person's sanity.

Early Morning Walk

Early in the morning, someone else was taking a walk
besides myself, lighting their way with a flashlight.
Yes, it was still dark outside,

the sun had yet to rise,
but I had no trouble seeing my way around
as I too walked through the neighborhood.

I could not understand the reason why anyone
needed a flashlight to find their way around.
Yes, the moon may have been out, but it

was unseen, now covered by a cloudy grey sky,
and even without the moonlight, I wondered
if she needed the light to look for

something she had lost earlier on her walk and
was retracing her steps back from her initial
route, or maybe she just didn't want to step on

any of the earth worms that were now resting on the
sidewalk from last night's rain, but that mystery
was partially solved as she turned around,

and saw she was wearing sunglasses. If they
had been night vision goggles, then there
wouldn't have been any need for the flashlight.

What a strange combination I thought, sunglasses
and a flashlight. It was like me eating a tuna fish
and chocolate syrup sandwich for lunch,

which by the way, is quite tasty.
I kept on walking, and did not ask, knowing
very well this mystery would remain unsolved.

Which Way Will the Wind Blow?

One-fourth of the neighbor's birch tree hung
over one yard to the north, and another fourth
hung over another neighbor's yard to the south,
with the rest of the tree hanging over the yard it was
intended to cover, the yard where its roots
were planted, and now stands tall along the fence
separating the three yards, though the two neighbors

had no ownership of the tree, each received an unwanted
share of the leaves when autumn rolled around.
Each hoping for an eastern wind to direct the leaves
to fall in the yard where they thought they all belonged,
but eastern breezes rarely seemed to happen,
so one wished for a northernly breeze, hoping
the majority of the leaves would go south

and the other neighbor hoped for a southernly breeze
where most of the leaves would find their way north,
anywhere but to each other's yards.
On occasion, each received their wish,
neither of them wanting to have to rake leaves
from a tree that did not grow in either of their yards,
but there they were, left with, piles of leaves

covering their grass, both tempted to
suck up the leaves with a vacuum then blow them
over the fence to where each thought they all belonged.
Which way would the wind blow?
One won yesterday, the other won today, but somehow,
neither felt like they had won at all as they stood in
their yards, raking up the leaves that had fallen.

Final Resting Spot

The neighbor's potted plant rested on
the deck in their backyard,
its leaves and stems brown,
its roots no longer requiring water
or leaves requiring sunlight from
the frost having taken its once flourishing life,
and now it is winter, covered by snow,
sitting next to deck furniture
that would not see any use for months,
until warmer weather had returned
and the snow had melted
allowing one to sit in comfort
without the use of a warm coat and hat.
As for the plant, there did not seem
to be any plans in the near future for a
celebration of life service, or any burial,
unless one calls the snow now covering it
as its final resting spot.

Unofficial Newspaper Carrier

I felt as if I was a newspaper carrier again
as I walked through the neighborhood seeing
many of the Wednesday ad sections stuffed in those
yellow, red, and white colored plastic bags still

laying in the snow, sometimes in the yard,
other times on the sidewalk or in the street,
missing their intended target of the driveway,
and then further ignored and neglected by

the customers they were intended for.
No one subscribed to the ads, but still,
they were faithfully delivered to those who didn't
already subscribe to the daily paper,

whether they wanted the ads or not, and it appeared
there was a fair share that probably didn't care
receiving them from all the bags still lying there,
and being the goody two shoes that I was, and not particularly

fond of seeing waste littering the neighborhood,
I picked up each bag holding the ads,
and tossed them into their driveways where
they were more visible, but knowing they still

might remain in the driveways all winter long.
Maybe I was helping, then maybe not,
but they were finally off the streets and lawns,
and at least one person felt better about that.

Searching for Land Mines

He held a metal detector, moving it back and
forth along the ground, but he wasn't searching
for land mines in a war zone. There were no shots
being fired, or bombs being dropped by planes.
He was making his search at the neighborhood

playground, maybe searching for long lost treasures
of gold doubloons buried in a treasure chest,
abandoned long ago by pirates, though the last
I had heard, Nebraska was nowhere near any
oceans or seas, but most likely searching

for loose change that escaped the prison that
once held them captive, the operator's fortune
to be found buried under the dirt and mulch, maybe
hoping to become the next self-made millionaire,
but how many of the children carried

change in their pockets, for there were no vending
machines in the playground that allowed them to
purchase any pop or candy, coins to be lost
as they coasted down the slides and crashed into
the ground, flying out as they swung on the swings,

or ran around playing various games within the park.
He may walk away in disappointment, but he wouldn't
be the first person not getting what they wanted in life.
If he only finds a penny, I suggest that he take it and
cherish it, a reward for his efforts no matter how small.

Pick-up Sticks

Even years later after playing my last game
of pick-up sticks from my childhood days,
those long-pointed colored sticks consisting
of reds, yellows, blues, and greens, where
each color indicated a different point value,
I was still picking up sticks, though the sticks
that I gathered no longer had any value.
They were the little branches that had fallen
from the neighbor's tree after strong winds
had blown through the neighborhood,
scattering them all over the backyard.
One by one, I pick up the little twigs and branches,
tempted to throw them back into the neighbor's yard,
but refrain, and instead, toss them into the trash can
all the while wishing they had planted a sturdier tree,
maybe an oak tree, where the branches were stronger
and less likely to fall from another blast of the wind.

The Life of a Dandelion

I noticed him holding a dandelion puller
as I strolled past him on my walk,
telling me that they all seemed to disappear

when he held it out in plain sight,
as if the dandelions could see what
tool of destruction he had in place for them,

or at least sensed its threat.
I just laughed and pointed one out to him
having no trouble finding them, especially

when they showed everyone their true colors,
their yellow flower in full bloom, just
hoping to live long enough to allow its flower

to dry up then wait for the wind to harvest
its seeds and distribute them over other
parts of the yard so its children too

would have a chance to grow and prosper.
As I continued my walk, I wished him good luck,
hoping that he succeeded with his dandelion infected yard.

Love and Hate

The sign posted on their front lawn stated
'Hate has no home here',
but I had a few words I wanted to add to it,
that all dandelions and other weeds
did have a home here.
It appeared there was a love connection as I
observed the overabundance of them in their yard.
They were a part of nature that was definitely not
hated and had found a welcoming home.
I too had no hate in my heart as I continued my walk,
especially for the people living there.
I had nothing but love for them.
I loved that they were not my next-door neighbors.

Shade of the Tree Stump

He finally figured it out,
that the tree stump wasn't going
to provide any shade in his front yard,
other than providing a little cover from the

sun for some insects and a few small birds,
if they chose to take up the stump's offer
over that of the healthy trees nearby.
The tree's life had been cut short

from a family of emerald ash borers, and finally
the tree was cut down, leaving only
a one-foot high stump, and now, many years later,
it was finally time for it to go too,

and it was just a matter of time
on how long it would take him to dig
the dirt around the stump and then take an axe
or chain saw to cut its roots attached to the earth.

It may become a summer long project,
and after this, who knows what
will take its place. Maybe some grass,
another tree, or left as a small hole with some

bare dirt to be covered later on by weeds
that decide to take refuge there,
yet another project that too may
take its time to complete.

Grooming

To some, our backyard could be considered
very boring with the lack of trees and bushes.
Oh, there were several planters
filled with flowers on the deck, but now,
the only thing growing in the yard was grass.

Two trees once enhanced the landscape,
but they did not survive, their lives cut short,
and the only remembrance of their existence
were from the mushrooms popping up from
the ground like pimples on a teenager's face

where the roots and trunk of the tree
once took strong hold in the earth.
I must admit though, being its caretaker,
that the grass was well-groomed each week,
making sure each blade of grass

was cut to a uniform height,
and if one was not a true believer
in what I tell as truth, I will loan them my ruler,
so they can measure each blade for them self,
and then see which one of us is crazy?

Plant Garden

I asked our neighbor what kind
of plant that was in her garden,
pointing to the tallest plant growing,
and she said that it was a weed,
then asked her what another kind of
plant was, and she also said it was a weed.
I asked one more time,
getting the same response.
I don't know if she got my hint or not,
but the plants kept firm root
in her garden, undisturbed,
some growing to three or four feet in height.
I guess they served a purpose,
filling up her garden with foliage.
I didn't know whether to call
it a flower garden with a lot of weeds,
or a weed garden with a few flowers,
so I will just call it a plant garden,
where any vegetation except vegetables
were allowed to grow.

Too Perfect

My wife looked out the kitchen window each day,
looking out at the potted plants on our neighbor's patio,
filled with bouquets of red flowers.
She made a comment that they couldn't be real,
they were too perfect, never seeming to change
in color or size, the flowers still in full bloom
weeks after being potted.
They have to be artificial she tells me,
since none of her plants had had a similar result.
She could have gotten the binoculars out
to see if she could determine if they were real or not,
or jumped the chain linked fence between our yards
when the neighbors were not at home to take a closer look,
or just ask when she happened to see one of them outside,
but instead, she just shakes her head.
They can't be real.

The Lumberjack

A new tree was planted after
a few insects had killed off the one prior,
still amazing me on how something so small
could kill off a tree so tall.
And now, the new tree,
ten feet tall and as thick as a pole vaulter's pole,
was slowly losing its leaves.

The countdown had been going on
for several weeks since the tree had
first been planted earlier this summer,
and now, only five green leaves remained,
still clinging onto life,
where maybe tomorrow the count would
be down to four leaves or less,
until finally, no leaves remained,
where only a scrawny trunk would be left
along with a few small branches
sticking out at the top.

His arborist skills seemed to be lacking,
having no luck with any of the trees
in his front yard, and soon,
another one looked set to die,
where once again, his lumber jack skills
would get put to good use.

Sunflowers

Birds could at times be sloppy eaters,
but I guess they were no different than
humans as they both sometimes spilled
food on the ground or the floor, though
humans tended to also spill food on their clothes.
While both types of food spilled would provide
new growth, the food of humans reaching
the floor would decay and grow moldy

while the seed that the birds dropped
from the bird feeders, falling
to the ground, took root,
growing taller than the poles holding the feeders,
hiding them in a jungle of their own,
a jungle of sunflowers
reaching for the sun.

Two-Face

The neighbors planted two evergreen trees,
one hundred feet from each other
in the two corners of their back yard.
One evergreen, still green and healthy,

and the other one reminding me of Batman's
villain, Two-Face, where one side of his face was normal,
while the other side was deformed from a fire,
with the second evergreen having a similar appearance,

with one side fully green and alive,
and the other side, brown and dead.
Did they give love and tender care to one tree,
and the other, ignore it, or spray it with harsh chemicals?

Two evergreens. Was one on the side of good,
and the other on the side of evil, good versus evil,
or was one just less fortunate,
like many of us in this world?

The Fall of the Bird Bath

The fall of the bird bath wasn't
anything like the fall of the Roman Empire,
but nonetheless, it toppled over

after three hours of a steady rainfall,
the ground caving in, slowly tilting the base,
until finally collapsing without the proper support.

The birds had no need for the bird bath
the day of the downpour, then,
there was plenty of water around,

but in the days after, they might need it
to quench their thirst, or to wash themselves up,
but right now, it lay on the ground, next to three

bird feeders, still standing, not affected by the rain.
No longer would there be any one stop shopping.
Now, the birds would need to make one additional

stop if they wished to eat and also clean up,
eating here in the backyard of the fallen bird bath,
followed by washing up in a yard two houses away,

one that only provided a bird bath.
Life just got a little tougher for our feathered friends,
one they can blame on the rain storm.

A Neighbor's Gift

After witnessing a neighbor losing
two trees over the past several years,
I thought about offering him the maple tree
that I had just pulled out of our flower garden

from our front yard this morning.
Yes, it was only eight inches in height,
but the size of each transplanted tree had
to start at some point in its life cycle.

The tree wasn't something I had planted,
but the wind had blown the seed into our yard,
travelling some distance from its mother's arms,
for there were no other maples trees on our block,

and nature continued taking care of it,
first finding earth, then rain and sunshine to nourish it.
I replanted the tree in a small paper cup filled with
a little top soil, giving it a fresh drink of water,

and placed the cup on the neighbor's front steps,
along with a note that said:
'The third time is a charm, take good care of your
new tree', signed, your neighborhood arborist.

The Self Assigned Leader

Several times a day, the neighbor's four
dogs were let out of the house so they
could take care of one of their basic needs,
with the younger female leading the pack,
heading out the door first, barking,
even though there wasn't
anything special going on outside,
when no other animals,
a rabbit or a squirrel, were nearby,
or one of the other neighbors out mowing
their grass, or just sitting on their
deck or patio trying to relax.
She was just letting everyone know
'Here I am, pay attention to me'.
Yes, here you are, once again.
I hear you, and each day that I am around
when you are let out of the house,
I see you looking for all the attention you
think you deserve as I listen to your voice,
a sound all too familiar.

Sharing Neighbors

I pulled my car out of garage onto the driveway
and noticed something on our front porch.
It wasn't any package that we had ordered,

but was tiny, and unwrapped.
The friendly neighborhood squirrel
had left us one of its acorns.

It must have had a good harvest
and wanted to share some of its wealth
with the rest of the neighbors.

I didn't look to see if anyone else
had this same gift left on their doorstep,
but it looked that it had learned a lesson

from one of our other neighbors who
from time to time left tomatoes and
green peppers at our front door.

It was nice to have neighbors who shared,
and I will have to return the favor, by putting some
field corn out for my new furry friend this winter.

Fall Clean-up

Spring clean-up time came,
nothing happened.
Summer clean-up time came,
nothing happened.
Fall clean-up time came,
life appeared,
something marked on the calendar,
clean up yard, if nice outside,
and feel like doing something useful.
One after one,
all the wild trees
growing along the fence,
each reaching heights of four to five feet,
cut a few inches
above ground level,
their roots still surviving,
giving them another chance
to continue next spring.
As each tree falls, timber is yelled.
Some weeds pulled,
other weeds survived,
waiting for winter to finish
the job started today.

Autumn Entertainment

I was easy to entertain come autumn time,
when the squirrels began getting ready for winter,
making multiple trips up and down the sidewalk
as if it were their highway through the neighborhood,
carrying acorns, one at a time, held in their teeth.

They had no trucks to help haul the acorns harvested,
and they were the only ones who cared, as those who
planted the trees for their shade, had no need for its food,
and were happy to see it disappear, and no shovels
were available to help them bury each one in the ground.

One by one, the squirrels carried each acorn,
going yard to yard, burying their winter's food supply,
and this, was more interesting than anything else going on,
hours of entertainment at hand,
watching the squirrels hard at work.

Backyard Forest

The neighbors had trees growing in some of the strangest
places in their back yard, trees not planted by them,
but instead planted by mother nature,
from the wind blowing seeds from other trees into their yard,

or birds carrying the seeds and dropping them
off like bombardiers in a war zone.
Three trees took root in the flower garden,
one especially designed to display only

their flowers, or so I thought was their intention.
A red sunset maple grew directly in one corner,
next to the two neighbors' fences,
a mulberry tree hugged another fence

near the middle of the border line,
and a honey locust thrived only inches away
from their storage shed.
Each of the trees now standing four to five feet tall,

so it wasn't like they had just magically
popped up from the ground and remained unnoticed.
Each spring, trees also sprung up in our yard,
pin oaks, maples, honey locusts, and birch trees,

using nature's same methods of distribution,
but I had no need for the trees like my neighbors,
and pulled them up after only growing
to a height of a couple inches,

tall enough to distinguish them from the grass.
I found no need for a forest growing in our yard,
as where our neighbors seemed quite happy
with theirs along with all the other vegetation

growing in other areas of their yard,
the neighborhood jungle, where I was
still waiting to hear Tarzan's famous yell
as the forest grew denser.

Mowing in the Dark

I wondered what was going on so late in
the day when I first heard the noise, a noise
of what sounded like a lawn mower running outside.

I just had to stick my head out the back door,
being one of those nosey neighbors, to see what was going on,
and confirm what I thought I had heard, since it was an

uncommon thing to do this late at night, but there she was,
mowing her grass, a half hour after the sun had set.
Maybe it had something to do with being a Friday

the Thirteenth with a full moon now out in plain display,
and something bad was going to happen
if she didn't get it done by the end of the day,

some superstitious thing about the day I was unaware of,
but there she was, out mowing her grass in the dark,
the lawn mower, complete with headlights.

Foot Traffic

Somedays, I had no trouble sleeping in,
maybe not as late as most others
accomplished on a regular basis,

but today after waking up,
I went for a walk knowing
it was supposed to be a nice day,

and since it was still early,
long before the sun would rise,
I didn't expect to see anyone else,

but three others were out walking their dogs,
and another two out for some exercise.
Traffic lights and stop signs were

not necessary to help manage the traffic flow.
We managed quite well without their assistance,
but in the end, I now knew

my idea wasn't truly unique,
but still, I didn't expect so many
others competing for the same sidewalks.

The Last Leaf

The snow blower, tuned-up earlier in the week,
one step in getting ready for winter, but now,
outside again, performing one final duty of fall,
running the lawn mower for the last time,

bagging up the fallen leaves in early November,
gloves and a winter coat, necessities.
The wind, uncooperative in my effort,
testing its strength as I continued my task,

knowing more leaves would end up making
a stop in the yard as I finished, a few from our tree,
the remaining, from a host of other
generous trees in the neighborhood,

each cooperating in an effort of recovering the ground just
cleaned up, somehow aware my obsession would not end
until all the leaves had disappeared, to another world,
a resting place, in another yard, anywhere but here, me,

not wanting to wait until spring returned to finish the job,
and having to think about it all winter long,
as the leaves lay in the yard,
wrapped in a blanket of winter's snow.

www.ingramcontent.com/pod-product-compliance
Lightning Source LLC
LaVergne TN
LVHW040048180726
843489LV00003B/1069